DOING WORK WITH SI

WORKING WITH
PULLEYS

RONALD MACHUT

PowerKiDS
press.
New York

Published in 2020 by The Rosen Publishing Group, Inc.
29 East 21st Street, New York, NY 10010

Copyright 2011; revised edition 2020

Editor: Elizabeth Krajnik
Book Design: Reann Nye

Photo Credits: Cover Roi Brooks/Shutterstock.com; p. 7 HW Photowork/ Shutterstock.com; p. 9 BBA Photography/Shutterstock.com; p. 10 Larissa Parr/ Shutterstock.com; p. 11 guillermo_celano/Shutterstock.com; p. 13 SasinTipchai/ Shutterstock.com; p. 15 M88/Shutterstock.com; p. 17 Steve Norman/Shutterstock. com; p. 18 bogdanhoda/Shutterstock.com; p. 19 designbydx/Shutterstock.com; p. 21 (top) Gyorgy Kotorman/Shutterstock.com; p. 21 (bottom) saulgranda/ Moment/Getty Images; p. 22 Brian A Jackson/Shutterstock.com.

Library of Congress Cataloging-in-Publication Data

Names: Machut, Ronald, author.
Title: Working with pulleys / Ronald Machut.
Description: New York : PowerKids Press, [2020] | Series: Doing work with
    simple machines | Includes bibliographical references and index.
Identifiers: LCCN 2018028492| ISBN 9781538343623 (library bound) | ISBN
    9781538345306 (pbk.) | ISBN 9781538345313 (6 pack)
Subjects: LCSH: Pulleys–Juvenile literature.
Classification: LCC TJ1103 .M33 2019 | DDC 621.8–dc23
LC record available at https://lccn.loc.gov/2018028492

Manufactured in the United States of America

CPSIA Compliance Information: Batch #CSPK19. For Further Information contact Rosen Publishing, New York, New York at 1-800-237-9932

CONTENTS

LEARNING ABOUT PULLEYS

You've probably used a pulley today without even knowing it. Did you help raise the flag at school? Did you ride your bike to the park? If you did, you've used a pulley! Many things use pulleys. Pulleys make it easier to raise and lower heavy loads. Pulleys are at work in buildings, in factories, and on farms, too!

Pulleys are simple machines. A simple machine is a **device** with few or no moving parts. These devices are used to modify, or change, motion and force to do work. The pulley is one of six simple machines.

MECHANICAL MARVELS

Some devices are made up of more than one simple machine. They're called **compound** machines. Tractors, cranes, and bulldozers are all compound machines.

INCLINED PLANE

LEVER

SCREW

WEDGE

PULLEY

WHEEL AND AXLE

The other simple machines are the inclined plane, the lever, the wedge, the wheel and **axle**, and the screw.

5

PULLEY PARTS

All pulleys are made up of a wheel that turns on an axle and a rope, chain, or **cable** that slides through a groove, or path, on the wheel. Wheels and axles may be made out of wood, metal, or plastic. The size of the wheel depends on where and how the pulley will be used.

The five kinds of pulleys include the fixed pulley, the movable pulley, the compound pulley, the block-and-tackle pulley, and the cone pulley. The most basic pulley is a fixed pulley. It's called a fixed pulley because the axle of the wheel is fixed, or stuck in place.

Pulleys can work on their own or together. Two or more pulleys that work together make a compound pulley.

PULLEYS AT WORK

←---------------------------------------→

Pulleys help us do work in three ways. Some pulleys change the direction of the force on the machine. Other pulleys work with belts or gears to share force from one system to another. Other pulleys are used to multiply the force to lift the heaviest loads.

Most simple machines provide mechanical advantage, which is the machine's ability to multiply the mechanical force applied to the load. Mechanical advantage is also called leverage. The higher the mechanical advantage, the less effort it takes to lift or lower a load with a pulley.

Pulleys make it possible for people to reach the top of a mountain in a short time. They can ride in cable cars, which are driven by fixed belt-and-pulley systems.

WHAT'S A FIXED PULLEY?

A fixed pulley is a pulley with an axle that's fixed in place. An example of a fixed pulley is the pulley used to raise a flag on a flagpole. A circle of rope runs through the pulley. The flag is clipped to one side of the rope. Then, the person pulls down on the other side of the rope, which raises the flag. The rope moves through the wheel's groove.

Even though this water well has a pulley, that doesn't mean it's easier to lift the weight of the bucket. The pulley simply changes the direction of the force applied to the rope from down to up.

The mechanical advantage of a fixed pulley is one, which means you must apply the same force to the rope that it takes to lift the flag. Fixed pulleys only change the direction of the force applied to the load.

WHAT'S A MOVABLE PULLEY?

A movable pulley is a pulley that has a movable axle. This kind of axle can move up, down, and side to side in space. On a movable pulley, one end of the rope that runs through the groove of the wheel is often fixed. The load is attached directly to the wheel, rather than to the rope like on a fixed pulley. This means that the wheel moves with the load.

An example of a movable pulley is a zip line. The pulley of a zip line moves along the rope, which is fixed at both ends, and the person acts as the load.

A movable pulley, such as a zip line, has a mechanical advantage of two. It doubles the force applied to the machine. This means that the person needs to apply less force to move the load.

WHAT'S A COMPOUND PULLEY?

Fixed and movable pulleys may be used together, with the rope running through the wheel of one pulley and then the other. A system of two or more pulleys working together in this way is called a compound pulley. Compound pulleys make it easier to lift heavy loads.

In a compound pulley, there's at least one fixed pulley and a movable pulley. There's more than one wheel and there may be more than one rope. The more pulleys you add, the easier it will be to lift the load. The more rope sections a compund pulley has, the greater its mechanical advantage is. However, it will also take longer to lift.

You can find many examples of compound pulleys at construction sites. These pulleys are used to lift very heavy objects.

ARCHIMEDES'S PULLEY

←-------------------------------------→

More than 2,000 years ago, a Greek **mathematician** and inventor named Archimedes **designed** the first block-and-tackle pulley. Archimedes lived in Sicily, an island that's part of present-day Italy. The block-and-tackle pulley, which was used by sailors and fishermen, may have been his most useful invention.

A block and tackle is a type of compound pulley that has two or more grooved wheels that spin on the same axle. This set of wheels is called a block. One fixed block and one movable block are tackled, or joined together by rope. Used together, the blocks can lift whole boats in and out of the water.

People often use block-and-tackle pulley systems to raise and lower the sails on sailboats. However, block-and-tackle pulley systems are also used to raise and lower entire ships.

MODERN PULLEYS

Pulleys play an important role, or part, in many **industries**. We need them to make, move, build, and fix the goods we buy, the buildings around us, and the roads and bridges on which we travel.

MECHANICAL MARVELS

In factories, on farms, and at seaports and airports, different kinds of cranes do all kinds of heavy lifting.

Sometimes ropes aren't strong enough to lift heavy loads. In those cases, cranes use metal chains instead of rope. The chain is looped around the wheels just like rope, but it's stronger.

People around the world use cranes to help them lift heavy loads. Crawler cranes work on buildings and roads. Floating cranes are used to build bridges and seaports. **Aerial** cranes carry loads to places that can't be reached by road. All these cranes use pulleys, powered by motors, to multiply force and make the job easier.

PULLEYS IN YOUR HOME

People have used pulleys to help them do work for a very long time. Many years ago, people used pulleys to lift water from wells and raise hay **bales** into **lofts**.

Pulleys are everywhere—even in your home! Window shades, which you can raise and lower with the pull of a string, show pulleys at work. The pulley in a window shade changes the direction of the force, so that when the cord is pulled down, the shade rises. A clothesline that moves between two fixed wheels is also a pulley at work. Pulleys in clotheslines also change the direction of the force.

MECHANICAL MARVELS

A clothesline has two pulleys. They are both fixed and the rope moves between them. Window shades also have a fixed pulley.

Pulleys can be used for a number of jobs. They're not always used to lift heavy things. Many years ago, people used chain boats or chain ferries, like the one pictured here, to cross rivers.

CLOTHESLINE

BIKES AND GEARS

Not all pulleys work the same way. The pulleys on a bicycle don't work like the pulleys on a crane. The two small gears and the chain that connects them make up the bicycle's pulley system. When you push down on a **pedal**, you're applying force to the front gear. The gear turns the chain, which turns the back gear. When the back gear turns, the back wheel turns, too. This pushes your bike forward.

Bike gears act like the pulleys in a clothesline and change the direction of the force. However, unlike the pulleys in a clothesline, bicycle gears drive the wheels of their system.

GLOSSARY

aerial: Occurring in the air.

axle: A bar on which a wheel or pair of wheels turns.

bale: A large, tight group of objects tied together.

cable: A strong rope often made of wires.

compound: Made up of two or more parts.

design: To create the plan for something.

device: A tool used for a certain purpose.

industry: A group of businesses that provide a certain product or service.

loft: An upper floor of a barn.

mathematician: A person who is an expert in mathematics.

pedal: A lever worked by a foot or feet.

INDEX

WEBSITES

Due to the changing nature of Internet links, PowerKids Press has developed an online list of websites related to the subject of this book. This site is updated regularly. Please use this link to access the list: www.powerkidslinks.com/dwsm/pulleys